MMO
181

MUSIC FOR SAXOPHONE QUARTET

* SOPRANO SAXOPHONE

Menuet - Boccherini (arr. Cailliet) ☐ Concertino (3rd Mvt.) - Ralph Hermann

Trois Conversations - Paul Pierné ☐ Fantasy & Fugue on O'Susanna (arr. Cailliet)

Introduction & Scherzo - Robert Clérisse ☐ The Gold Rush Suite - Jack Marshall

Menuet

B♭ Soprano Saxophone

SIDE A - BAND 1

Boccerini
(arr. Cailliet)

181

2

Trois Conversations

I Conversation Amusante

Bb Soprano Saxophone
SIDE A - BAND 2

Paul Pierné

181
By courtesy of Editions Billaudot, 14, rue de L'Echiquier, Paris 10, France
Owners and Publishers

II Conversation Sentimentale

SIDE A - BAND 3

181

4

III Conversation Animée

Concertino (3rd Mvt.)

B♭ Soprano Saxophone

Ralph Hermann

We wish to express our appreciation to composer Ralph Hermann for making available to us his original manuscript of the Concertino-3rd mvt. The printed score and parts may be obtained from Podium Music, Inc., 4 Broadway, Valhalla, New York 10595.

7

Introduction & Scherzo

B♭ Soprano

Robert Clérisse

By courtesy of Alphonse Leduc & Co., 175, rue Saint-Honore - Paris 1er, France
Owners and Publishers

Fantasy & Fugue on O'Susanna

B♭ Soprano Saxophone

(arr. Cailliet)

Note to the Director

This suite of 7 musical numbers associated with the '49ers was conceived with the Hollywood Saxophone Quartet in mind. Jack Marshall, the composer, dedicated the suite to that peerless ensemble and scored it for 4 saxophones — B-flat Soprano, E-flat Alto, B-flat Tenor and E-flat Baritone. The Hollywood Saxophone Quartet recorded the suite, and that recording is available in the album "Warm Winds" — Liberty LRP 3047.

Laymen and musicians who have heard the recording have found the music to be sprightly and refreshing, and their enthusiasm for the music has increased with repeated hearings.

Because of the music's appeal and its suitability for woodwind ensembles and quartets, the publisher asked Mr. Marshall for permission to make the suite available not only to other saxophone quartets but also to other combinations of instruments of the woodwind family. Mr. Marshall agreed to the proposal, and this publication is the result.

The full score is in concert pitch and shows the 4 voices exactly as Jack Marshall wrote them for the Hollywood ensemble. The 9 instrumental parts are in the appropriate keys for the individual instruments and are distributed thus:

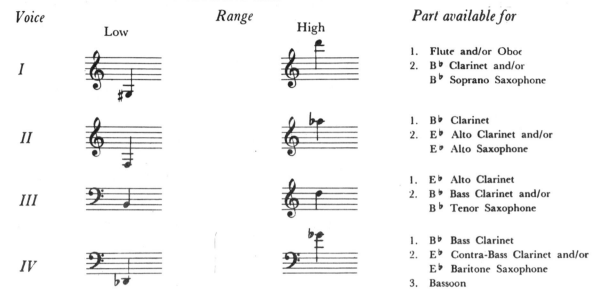

Voice	Range	Part available for
I	Low — High	1. Flute and/or Oboe 2. B♭ Clarinet and/or B♭ Soprano Saxophone
II	Low — High	1. B♭ Clarinet 2. E♭ Alto Clarinet and/or E♭ Alto Saxophone
III	Low — High	1. E♭ Alto Clarinet 2. B♭ Bass Clarinet and/or B♭ Tenor Saxophone
IV	Low — High	1. B♭ Bass Clarinet 2. E♭ Contra-Bass Clarinet and/or E♭ Baritone Saxophone 3. Bassoon

In 8 places Voice I is below the range of the flute and oboe. In those 8 instances Mr. Marshall's original scoring for Voice I appears in large-sized notes in the Flute-Oboe part, and the part for Voice II (which is within the range of those two instruments) appears in cue-sized notes. Also, in those 8 instances this practice has been reversed in the instrumental parts for Voice II, i.e., the second voice is in large-sized notes and the first voice in cue-sized notes.

Specifically the cue-sized notes appear in these 8 places:

    3. CALIFORNIA STAGE COACH
           Letter D - 4 measures
    5. WHAT WAS YOUR NAME IN THE STATES?
           Letter F - 1 measure
           Letter G - 1 measure
           Letter H - 1 measure
           Letter J - 6 measures
    6. LOUSY MINER   Letter C - 2nd measure
    7. JOE BOWERS and CALIFORNIA BANK ROBBERS
           Letter E - 4 measures
           Letter I - 15 measures

In those instances in which Voice IV is below the range of the B-flat Bass Clarinet, the octave above has been added in cue-sized notes.

This use of cues makes it possible for the suite to be played in its entirety by any quartet of instruments selected from the above chart. It also enables the director to experiment with combinations of tonal colors indigenous to the woodwind family.

Complete score and parts available for
Saxophone Quartet and/or Woodwind Ensemble
from Shawnee Press, Inc., Delaware Water Gap, Pa. 18327

Score — $3   Quartet — $6   Ensemble — $10   Extra parts — $1 ea.

181

Program Notes

THE GOLD RUSH SUITE was written for the Hollywood Saxophone Quartet using the themes of songs that were played and sung in California's 1850 gold rush days.

1 SWEET BETSY FROM PIKE — Among the thousands starting the long trip across the plains to California with gold dust in their eyes, was Sweet Betsy and her lover Ike. This is a ballad of their trip beginning from Independence, Missouri and ending at Placerville, California.

2 THE DAYS OF '49 — About 1858 two pocket song books, "Puts' Original California Songster" and "Puts' Golden Songster" were published in Sacramento. Old Puts' songs were as wild and lusty as the audience that listened to them, and none was better liked than "The Days of '49".

3 CALIFORNIA STAGE COACH — The song describes the rigors of an early stage coach ride; maybe from the gold fields to one of the hastily constructed opera houses in San Francisco, where the free spending miners paid for entertainment.

4 USED UP MAN — This is the story of a miner who had seen better days. No food, no women, nowhere to live and what's worse... no g o l d.

5 WHAT WAS YOUR NAME IN THE STATES? — Nothing in the new world before had ever called together such a strange medley of men as this golden army. There were rich men, poor men, beggar men and thieves. And many of the latter had aliases which explains the above title.

6 LOUSY MINER — The title of this song is in no way a reflection on the man's mining ability, but rather refers to the fact that he's just naturally unwashed and covered with lice.

7 "JOE BOWERS" and "CALIFORNIA BANK ROBBERS" — Two themes are used and inter-twined in this last movement of the suite. Joe Bowers was an old prospector and the California Bank Robbers were "robbers" only in a legal way. They were the men who loaned the prospectors money at a very high rate of interest. They struck gold in their own way.

JACK MARSHALL

About the Composer

Jack Marshall was born in Kansas and raised in California. After four years in the army he returned to the University of Southern California, graduating with Bachelor's and Master's degrees in engineering. He worked his way through college playing the guitar, then continued on in music, studying orchestration and composition privately. For eight years he was under contract to M-G-M Studios. He has recorded hit records with many popular artists: Doris Day, Dean Martin, Pat Boone, Ella Mae Morse, Tab Hunter, Bing Crosby, Gale Storm.

More recently his skillful and imaginative arrangements for Peggy Lee's Capitol recordings have been widely hailed, as have his own Capital albums featuring unusual combinations of instruments ("18th Century Jazz"; "Soundsville!").

Jack Marshall also has composed several notable cinema scores, including that for the United Artists production "Thunder Road".

15

The Gold Rush Suite

B♭ Soprano Saxophone

1. Sweet Betsy from Pike

Jack Marshall

17

2. The Days of '49

3. California Stage Coach

4. Used up Man

5. What Was Your Name in the States?

6. Lousy Miner

7. Joe Bowers and California Bank Robbers

COMPLETE MUSIC MINUS ONE
Brass CATALOGUE

ALTO SAXOPHONE

MMO 1045	Strangers In The Night/Downtown/Ipanema/etc. Bluesette/Call Me/I Want To Hold Your Hand/etc.
MMO 1052	Dolly/Ipanema/Bluesette/Sunny/One Note Samba/ San Francisco/What The World Needs Now/etc.
MMO 1053	Stella By Starlight/Out Of Nowhere/Black Magic/ Phoenix/Moon River/Alfie/The Nearness Of You/San Francisco/Sunny/I Remember You
MMO 1058	Bacharach For Instrumentalists
MMO 4006	For Saxes Only
MMO 4017	Lee Konitz Sax Duets
MMO 4022	20 Dixieland Classics
MMO 4027	20 Rhythm Backgrounds
MMO 4031	Swingin' The Classics
MMO 4036	Two Much! 16 Jazz Duets
MMO 4037	Sweet Sixteen Jazz Duets
MMO 4043	How About You?
MMO 4046	Makin' Whoopee!
MMO 4051	'Little Jazz Duets' minus Alto Sax
MMO 4056	Two by Four Jazz Duets in the Round
MMO 6005	Music For Brass Ensemble
MMO 6019	Ewald, Bach, Pezel, Franck, Handel, Purcell
MMO 7022	Easy Solos For Alto Sax
MMO 7027	Easy Alto Sax Solos #2
MMO 7032	More Easy Alto Sax Solos
MMO 7037	Easy Classics For Alto Sax
MMO 7044	Have Band — Will Travel
MMO 7051	Band Aids
MMO 7057	Popular Concert Favorites
MMO 7061	Solos With Concert Band
MMO 7065	Concert Band Classics
MMO 7069	Sousa Marches minus Alto Sax
MMO 7080	On Parade (Sousa & others)
MMO 7086	Concert Band Encores
MMO TP 4	Basic Saxophone Studies for the student

FRENCH HORN

MMO 105	Beethoven/Mozart Piano—With Quintets
MMO 149	Beeth., Haydn, Colomer, Mozart, Lefebvre Quintets
MMO 155	Reicha, Barthe, Haydn, Lefebvre Quintets
MMO 161	Mozart, Haydn, Colomer, Deslandres, Danzi
MMO 173	Bach/Haydn/Mozart/Koepke/Klughardt/Balay
MMO 6002	Music For Brass Ensemble
MMO 6009	Mozart: 12 Sonatas for 2 Horns
MMO 6010	Solos For The French Horn Player
MMO 6016	Ewald, Bach, Pezel, Franck, Handel, Purcell
MMO 6020	Mozart: French Horn Concerti K. 417/447
MMO 7046	Have Band—Will Travel
MMO 7053	Band—Aids
MMO 7089	Concert Band Encores

MELLOPHONE

MMO 6005	Music For Brass Ensemble
MMO 6019	Ewald, Bach, Pezel, Franck, Handel, Purcell

TENOR SAXOPHONE

MMO 1044	Strangers In The Night/Downtown/Ipanema/ Call Me/I Want To Hold Your Hand/etc.
MMO 1052	Dolly/Ipanema/Bluesette/Sunny/One Note Samba/ San Francisco/What The World Needs Now/etc.
MMO 1053	Stella By Starlight/Out Of Nowhere/Black Magic/ Phoenix/Moon River/Alfie/The Nearness Of You/San Francisco/Sunny/I Remember You
MMO 1058	Bacharach For Instrumentalists
MMO 4006	For Saxes Only!
MMO 4017	Lee Konitz Sax Duets
MMO 4021	20 Dixieland Classics
MMO 4026	20 Rhythm Backgrounds
MMO 4030	Swingin' The Classics
MMO 4038	Tenor Sax Jazz Duets
MMO 4039	Tenor Duets 16 Jazz Duets
MMO 4042	Solo Spotlight 12 rhythm backgrounds
MMO 4045	Fools Rush In + 11 other standards
MMO 4052	'Little Jazz Duets' minus Tenor Sax
MMO 4057	Two by Four. Jazz Duets in the Round
MMO 7045	Have Band—Will Travel
MMO 7052	Band—Aids
MMO 7088	Concert Band Encores

TROMBONE

MMO 1046	Strangers In The Night/Downtown/Ipanema/ Bluesette/Call Me/I Want To Hold Your Hand/etc.
MMO 1052	Dolly/Ipanema/Bluesette/Sunny/One Note Samba/ San Francisco/What The World Needs Now/etc.
MMO 1053	Stella By Starlight/Out Of Nowhere/Black Magic/ Phoenix/Moon River/Alfie/The Nearness Of You/San Francisco/Sunny/I Remember You
MMO 1058	Bacharach For Instrumentalists
MMO 4023	20 Dixieland Classics
MMO 4028	20 Rhythm Backgrounds
MMO 4044	12 Rhythm Backgrounds To Standards
MMO 4047	'. . . they laughed when I sat down to play'
MMO 4060	'Little Jazz Duets'
MMO 4061	Two by Four Jazz Duets in the Round
MMO 6003	Music For Brass Ensemble
MMO 6007	Solos For The Trombone—16 selections
MMO 6011	Blazhevich Trombone Duets Volume 1
MMO 6012	Blazhevich Trombone Duets Volume 2
MMO 6017	Ewald, Bach, Pezel, Franck, Handel, Purcell
MMO 7024	Easy Solos For The Trombone
MMO 7029	Easy Trombone Solos #2
MMO 7034	More Easy Trombone Solos
MMO 7039	Easy Classics For Trombone
MMO 7047	Have Band—Will Travel
MMO 7054	Band Aids
MMO 7090	Concert Band Encores
MMO TP 5	Basic Trombone Studies for the student

TRUMPET

MMO 136	First Chair Trumpet Solos
MMO 137	Bach: Brand. #2/Torelli/Stradella/Manfredini/ Purcell
MMO 1044	Strangers In The Night/Downtown/Ipanema/ Bluesette/Call Me/I Want To Hold Your Hand/etc.
MMO 1052	Dolly/Ipanema/Bluesette/Sunny/One Note Samba/ San Francisco/What The World Needs Now/etc.
MMO 1053	Stella By Starlight/Out Of Nowhere/Black Magic/ Phoenix/Moon River/Alfie/The Nearness Of You/San Francisco/Sunny/I Remember You
MMO 1058	Bacharach For Instrumentalists
MMO 4010	For Horns Only!
MMO 4021	20 Dixieland Classics
MMO 4026	20 Rhythm Backgrounds
MMO 4030	Swingin' The Classics
MMO 4038	Tenor Sax Jazz Duets
MMO 4041	Trumpet Duets In Jazz
MMO 4042	Solo Spotlight 12 rhythm backgrounds
MMO 4045	Fools Rush In
MMO 4054	'Little Jazz Duets'
MMO 4059	Two by Four Jazz Duets in the Round
MMO 6001	Music For Brass Ensemble
MMO 6006	Solos For The Trumpet Player
MMO 6008	Haydn/Telemann/Fasch Concerti
MMO 6013	Elementary my dear student Arban Duets Vol. 1
MMO 6014	Arban Revisited Arban Duets Vol. 2
MMO 6015	Ewald, Bach, Pezel, Franck, Handel, Purcell, Brade
MMO 7023	Easy Solos For Trumpet
MMO 7028	Easy Trumpet Solos #2
MMO 7033	More Easy Trumpet Solos
MMO 7038	Easy Classics For Trumpet
MMO 7043	Have Band—Will Travel
MMO 7050	Band—Aids
MMO 7058	Popular Concert Favorites
MMO 7062	Solos With Concert Band
MMO 7066	Concert Band Classics
MMO 7070	Sousa Marches minus Trumpet
MMO 7081	On Parade (Sousa & others)
MMO 7087	Concert Band Encores
MMO TP 3	Basic Trumpet Studies for the student

TUBA

MMO 6004	Music For Brass Ensemble
MMO 6018	Ewald, Bach, Pezel, Franck, Handel, Purcell, Brade

MUSIC MINUS ONE. 50 EXECUTIVE BLVD. ELMSFORD, NY 10523-1325